Reading American History

The Pony Express

Written by Melinda Lilly
Illustrated by Lori Kiplinger Pandy

Educational Consultants

Kimberly Weiner, Ed.D
Betty Carter, Ed.D

Rourke
Publishing LLC
Vero Beach, Florida 32963

www.rourkepublishing.com

**Many thanks to my family, especially Scott and Sierra,
who sometimes believe in me more than I do myself.
—L. K. P.**

Designer: Elizabeth J. Bender

Library of Congress Cataloging-in-Publication Data

Lilly, Melinda.
   The Pony Express / Melinda Lilly; illustrated by Lori Kiplinger Pandy.
      p. cm. — (Reading American history)
   Summary: A simple introduction of how the riders of the Pony Express delivered the
   mail from Saint Joseph, Missouri, to Sacramento, California.
   ISBN 1-58952-364-4
   1. Pony express—Juvenile literature. [1. Pony express.] I. Pandy, illus. II. Title.

HE6375.P65 L55 2002
383'.143'0973—dc21   2002017046

Cover Illustration: A young Pony Express rider in the Rocky Mountains

Printed in the USA

Time Line

Help students follow this story by introducing important events in the Time Line.

1847   Mail service to the Pacific Coast

1848   California Gold rush begins.

1860   The Pony Express carries mail from Missouri to California.

1860   Abraham Lincoln elected president.

1861   Telegraph lines cross the West from Missouri to California.

1861   The Pony Express goes bankrupt.

1869   Railroads span the continent.

The news has to get to **California**, fast.

The **Pony Express** rider grabs the news and the mail.

He puts them in his bag.

The Pony Express and the mail

He jumps on his **horse**.

"Yah!"

A **storm** is coming.

Off he goes!

The snow pelts him as he rides.

The Pony Express keeps going.

He rides fast.

He stops just to get a new horse.

The Pony Express had many horses.

He races past **robbers**.

Robbers try to rob the Pony Express.

He is tired.

A new rider takes the news and the mail.

At last, the rider gets some rest.

The Pony Express rides day and night.

At night

The last rider reaches California.

The people wave hello.

The Pony Express has come from **Missouri** in just seven days.

Greeting the Pony Express

California gets the news.
Abraham Lincoln will be the next
president!

The Pony Express rider shares the news.

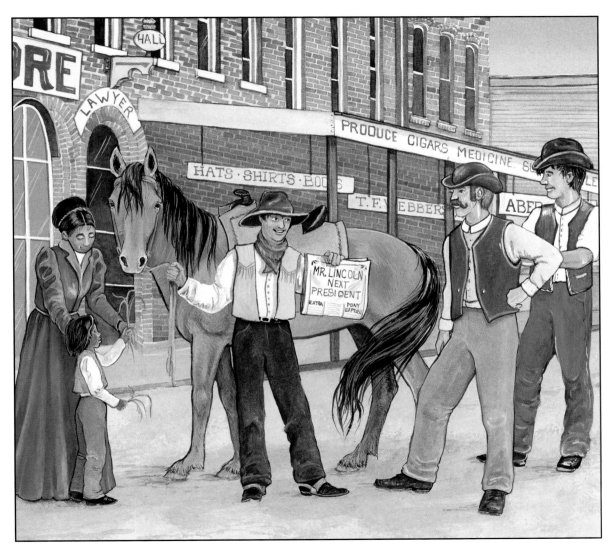

Word List

California (kal uh FORN yuh)—A U. S. state on the Pacific coast

horse (HORS)—A large animal with four legs and hard hoofs

Lincoln, Abraham (LING ken, AY breh ham)—U. S. president during the Civil War, Abraham Lincoln held the office from 1861 to 1865.

Missouri (mih ZOO ree)—A state in the middle region of the U. S.

Pony Express (POH nee ik SPRESS)—From 1860 to 1861, the Pony Express carried mail and news from Missouri to California.

president (PREZ ih dent)—The chief executive of the United States

robbers (ROB erz)—People who steal

storm (storm)—Rain, snow, or hail accompanied by winds

Books to Read

Kroll, Steven. *Pony Express!* Scholastic, 2000.

Marvis, B. *Pony Express*. Chelsea House, 2002.

Quasha, Jennifer. *The Pony Express: Hands-On Projects About Early Communication*. PowerKids, 2001.

Williams, Jean. *The Pony Express*. Compass Point Books, 2002.

Websites to Visit

www.xphomestation.com/

www.ci.st-joseph.mo.us/pony.html

www.sfmuseum.org/hist1/pxpress.html

http://comspark.com/chronicles/ponyexpress.shtml

www.stjosephmuseum.org/PonyExpress/history.html

Index